The Baker's Dozen Cookbook Series
Volume 3

Best Bagels

Marcy Goldman

River Heart Press
Montreal, Canada

The Baker's Dozen Series, Volume Three
Best Bagels

Text and Recipes by Marcy Goldman

River Heart Press 2021
Montreal, Canada

All rights reserved. No part of this book may be used or reproduced, in any form or by any means without prior written permission of the author/publisher, excepting brief quotations in connection with reviews written specifically for inclusion in magazines, newspapers and electronic media.

Marcy Goldman is a cookbook author, master baker and host of the www.BetterBaking.com

Library and Archives Canada in Publication
ISBN 978-1-927936-38-2 Print Book
ISBN 978-1927936-32-0 E Book

Goldman, Marcy
The Baker's Dozen Series, Volume Three
Marcy Goldman Presents The Baker's Dozen Volume Three, Best Bagels

Other Books by Marcy Goldman
A Treasury of Jewish Holiday Baking Whitecap Books 2007
The New Best of Betterbaking.com Whitecap Books 2007
When Bakers Cook, River Heart Press 2013
A Passion for Baking, River Heart Press 2014
The Baker's Four Seasons River Heart Press 2014
Love and Ordinary Things River Heart Press 2014
The Newish Jewish Cookbook River Heart Press 2019

Marcy Goldman's The Baker's Dozen Series River Heart Press
All Available in E-book or Print format

The Baker's Dozen Volume One Best Holiday Cookies 2016
The Baker's Dozen Volume Two Best Biscotti 2017
The Baker's Dozen Volume Three Best Bagels 2021
The Baker's Dozen Volume Four Best Scones 2021

Table of Contents

The Baker's Dozen Best Bagels 1

New York Style Water Bagels 7

Everything Bagel 9

Cinnamon Raisin Whole-Wheat Bagels 11

The Legend of Montreal Bagels 12

Montreal Bagels 15

Caramel Apple Bagels 17

Dark Rye and Currant Pumpernickel Bagels 19

Pumpkin Cranberry Bagels 21

Spelt & Whole Wheat and Flax Seed Bagels 23

Rosemary Sea Salt Bagels 25

Stuffed Cheddar Cheese Bagels 27

Wild Blueberry Bagels 29

Twisted Bagel Bread 31

Old Fashioned Onion Bialys 33

Bonus Free Recipes Offer 35

The Baker's Dozen
Best Bagels

"Az men est op dem baigel bleibt in keshene der lock"
If you eat a bagel, only the hole remains in your pocket

A Bagel Love Affair

Over the years, I've made a lot of bagels. Seriously: a lot of bagels. And that includes both my personal life (as a bagel fan and home baker) as well as a professional baker and food writer, contributing bagel features for food magazines, in print as well as online and newspapers. In fact, my first bagel feature was way back when, for the *New York Times*. I pitched a piece on Montreal bagels (and why I think they are better or different than New York bagels). Somehow I convinced my sceptical New York Times food editor at the time to take the story. They published my story, along with some photos my brother took and the recipe for famed Montreal bagels that I had worked on for ages. So trust me when I say my love affair with bagels goes way back!

As with pizza, bagels are a unique food that has crossed the food and culture line to mainstream status. Good with anything: jam, cream cheese, sandwich fillings or simply toasted with butter, bagels have only fans. I honestly never met anyone who didn't like bagels. Show me someone who doesn't like bagels and I'll show you someone who has never had one (or had a good one).

On the Jewish table, bagels are inevitable, comforting, and always appropriate. They're served at the holidays (especially at Yom Kippur, breaking the fast) and they're front and centre at births of new babies where bagels represent the continuity of life.

So where did bagels, aka an unassuming boiled yeast bun with the hole in its centre come from? Bagels were brought to North America by European Jewish immigrants. In Leo Rosten's book, *The Joys of Yiddish* the author notes the first printed usage of the word "bagel" is in the "Community Regulations for Cracos, which stated that the item was given as a gift to women in childbirth.

In *Deli*, (Sue Kreitzman, Harmony Books, N.Y. 1985) there's a quote pinned down to a 1946 newspaper article describing bagels as a "doughnut with rigor mortis", a most unfortunate misconception. The point however, is well-taken: oven-fresh bagels are worth a king's ransom, while stale ones can in act be used as a weapon or paperweight. So freeze 'em or eat 'em but don't let fresh bagels hang around. (That said here's some extra good news: homemade bagels somehow stay fresh far longer – all the more reason to make your own).

Bagels: The Whole Truth

As bakery trends come and go and few, only a merited ones become classics. Carrot cakes and chocolate chip cookies come to mind. But so do bagels. In part we can thank bagel maven Murray Lender's diligent marketing of this specialty product to the masses which insured national bagel exposure (and consequent familiarity beyond New York City) paving the way for the bagel entrepreneurs ever since.

Bagels have retained their popularity for the longest time and it doesn't take a rocket scientist to figure why. Bagels are innately low in fat, low in sugar, a diet-friendly complex carbohydrate (if you use whole-grains in your homemade bagels), as easy on the budget as they are (if eaten in moderation) on the bulge, suitable with everything, and as comforting as an old friend. Neither a bread nor a roll but a unique hybrid, a bagel is at once fragrant, crusty, amber-colored, and hearty looking. A hot bagel, along with its unrivalled aroma, fortunately, tastes as good as it looks: chewy yet crisp, honest, down-to-earth, wheaty taste, satisfying in their simplicity. On their own, bagels are sublime, but when used as the foundation for a multitude of toppings (e.g. cream cheese spread, hummus), they become a meal in themselves. Plus bagels have one other unique trait they only share with pretzels: bagels are boiled first and then baked. I for one, rather like that defining characteristic.

Why Make Your Own Bagels?

Bagels are fun, easy as pie, and, I won't lie: homemade ones are as good if not better than store-bought – at least I think my recipes will make that last statement a fact beyond dispute! (Of course you'll have to make some to be convinced). Nothing but nothing is as simple to make, **not** at all time-consuming and yields something so utterly sensational. Plus you can make any flavour you like, any size and use the best ingredients you trust (organic bread flour anyone?).

No Special Equipment, No Special Ingredients – and You Can Still Have the Best Bagels!

To make great bagels, you don't have to live in New York nor do you need a special oven, special mixer or even a lot of time and you don't even need to be an experienced baker. Thanks to the dough hooks, mixers, bread machines, bread flour, and great yeast homemade yet authentic homemade bagels are a 90-minute reality. The only thing you really need is a great bagel recipe and for that I got you covered!

What you should keep in mind about bagels is that bagel dough should be very stiff to the point of slickness (all the better to hold their shape as they are formed, kettled and baked). Unlike bread, which have two decent rise periods, bagels are barely allowed to rest, let alone enjoy a leisurely rise before they are thrown into a simmering water bath. Bagels inflate when they are kettled (the boiling bath) and have a final last gasp in the oven before the yeast finally dies and the bagel structure is set. But most of the rise is in that brief stint in the simmering kettle water.

If you allow bagels to rise too much before being shaped, the dough becomes slack and the doughy rings can't retain their shape in the subsequent boiling water bath. Also, you lose that characteristic, appealing denseness. Kettling the bagels is also what gives bagels their shine. Just remember, the water should be just a healthy simmer (not a rolling boil) which promotes the proper gelatinization of the outer crust.

Ingredients

You can make bagels from ingredients sitting in your pantry and still achieve wonderful bagels. But using dedicated bagel ingredients - strong bread flour, fragrant, whole-meal pumpernickel flour (which is rye flour, ground germ, berry and all), baker's caramel, malt syrup or malt powder, to name a few, will render absolutely superlative bagels. Here's the run down on some bagel basics, in terms of ingredients:

Water

People love to think that New York Bagels are special because of the water in that city. But the water in every city is different, as is the air, the climate, the humidity etc. And all these things affect bagels but again, what's key is to start with a good recipe and sound handling. The water you use will not make or break an otherwise superlative bagel, but you are welcome to use bottled (non-chlorinated water).

Malt

Malt gives bagels their mystique and marvellous flavor and is long a part of bagel history in America. Malt can be called malt powder, malt flour, dry malt or malt syrup. It comes in powder form as diastatic malt or non-diastatic varieties if you get it from a bakery supply company like King Arthur Baker's Flour or from a bulk ingredients store (even a bagel bakery will sometimes sell you some). You can also find malt syrup in beer brewing stores. It doesn't much matter which malt you use, *all* malt will all work for bagels (although dry malt is easier to work with than the syrup). When it comes to malt, some professional bakers swear by it and others deny it has any business in their bagels, plus it's an ingredient that home bakers often have to sleuth out. I find malt assists with browning, feeds the yeast, and adds authentic bagel flavour. This all said, if you want to get started right away and don't have malt on hand, use brown sugar instead.

Bread Flour and Other Flours

Bread flour is what I prefer for bagels. Bread flour has the sufficient presence of gluten, the flour's protein, to give a finished bagel its chewiness and crustiness. Choose *unbleached* bread flour in your supermarket or bulk food store. If you're really impatient and don't have bread flour on hand, you can use all-purpose flour.

Dark rye, pumpernickel, light rye, coarse rye are all descriptions of rye flour granulations. Usually dark, coarse, and pumpernickel mean similar things and are interchangeable.

If you can, try and get stone ground rye as this has the most flavor.

Yeast

Bagels use comparatively little yeast and these recipes work with either active dry yeast or instant or fast-rising yeast. I just happen to prefer instant yeast and these recipes were tested with that. I use Saf, Fermipan or if that's not available, I use Red Star or Fleischmann's. Just remember that less yeast makes chewy, dense bagels and *more* yeast, will make puffier bagels that are more like bread or rolls. If you have access to fresh yeast, that's ideal - most recipes would work with 3/4 ounce fresh yeast to replace the dry, instant yeast called for.

Baker's Caramel

Baker's caramel (which I use for pumpernickel bagels) is a natural coloring agent that gives pumpernickel and dark rye breads their hearty hue. Essentially it is caramelized sugar and it resembles dark brewed coffee. A runner-up ingredient if you don't have Baker's Caramel on hand would be Kitchen Bouquet, found in supermarkets in the gravy and soup mixes section.

Bagel Techniques

As with most yeast breads, bagel dough can be made almost any way you require, depending on your preference of kneading procedures or equipment on hand. But since bagels are made from a dense, slick dough, it's best to knead with a dough hook or bread machine. By hand, kneading bagel dough is a rigorous task because it takes more kneading muscle to activate the gluten in bread flour (which is in most bagel recipes).

Bread machines are one of your best bets, churning out superb bagel dough and as trouble-free as you would want. The non-stick baking pan in bread machines enables bagel dough to absorb more flour more readily and this yields optimally stiff bagel dough. When using a bread machine, just dump ingredients in same order as given (avoid having salt touch yeast, however) and put machine on Dough mode or program. As soon as the dough is mixed and had its final knead *remove* it from the machine and continue on with the recipe. Don't allow the dough to sit and rise in the machine, awaiting the cycle's customary completion.

While most bread machines stipulate a 3-cup capacity for the dough making capacity is greater and most machines can easily manipulate 4-6 cups of flour well. I often make several batches of bagels, using two bread machines to make consecutive batches of dough. This leaves my hands free to form and shape bagels as well as boil and bake them since the bread machine handles the dough-making task.

That's about all you need to know, so happy bagel making! And don't forget to have plenty of butter and cream cheese on hand (and also please remember – make lots of bagels. They freeze like a dream!)

Baker's Tip #1

New York Style Water Bagels

New York Water Bagels are usually quite big which is part of their appeal. So be generous with the dough portions and bake them to a toasty brown for an appealing colour and taste.

New York Style Water Bagels

These sassy bagels are also known as water bagels. If the secret ingredient, as New Yorkers brag, is the water, then we out-of-towners are out of luck. Minus the Hudson River, these bagels are still as authentic as you can get without buying them from H&H Bagels!

1 1/2 cups warm water
1 tablespoon instant yeast
1 tablespoon sugar
1 tablespoon oil
2 teaspoons malt powder, optional
2 teaspoons salt
4 1/2 - 5 1/2 cups bread flour

Kettle Water
6 quarts water
2 tablespoons malt syrup or honey, optional
1 teaspoon salt

Finishing Touches
Cornmeal, optional
Sesame, poppy seeds

In a mixer bowl, whisk together water, yeast, and sugar. Let stand a couple of minutes to allow yeast to dissolve. Briskly whisk in in oil, malt and one cup of flour. Add salt, then most of remaining flour, kneading 10-12 minutes to make a very stiff dough, adding in more flour if required.

Cover with a tea towel and let dough rest on a board about 15 minutes. Meanwhile, line two large baking sheets with baking parchment and sprinkle generously with corn meal. Fill a large pot two-thirds full with water; add the malt syrup and salt. Bring water to a gentle boil. Preheat oven to 450° F.

Divide dough into 10 sections and form into 10 inch long strips. Roll the ends together to seal and make a ring. Place on a very lightly floured surface near your stove. Let bagels rest 15-20 minutes.

Prepare two more baking sheets - line one with a kitchen towel and the other with parchment paper which has been sprinkled with cornmeal, if desired. Reduce water to simmer and add bagels a few at a time. Allow to come to surface and simmer thirty seconds. Turn over and cook other side about 45 seconds more. Place on prepared towel-lined baking sheet. Leave plain or sprinkle with sesame or poppy seeds.

Place in oven, reduce heat to 425° F. and bake until done, about 17-22 minutes, turning bagels once, when almost baked.

Makes 10

Baker's Tip #2

Everything Bagel

The best part of Everything Bagels is the topping so make sure you're roll these bagels very generously in the topping. Everything Topping comes pre-made or make your own by combining equal portions of poppy seeds, sesame seeds and dehydrated garlic and/or onions.

Everything Bagel

This is one of my favorite bagels since it's a classic bagel but topped with irresistible, zesty toppings. It's full of flavour and perfect for any sort of sandwich to serve at a festive brunch.

1 1/2 cups warm water
1 tablespoon instant yeast
1 tablespoon sugar
1 tablespoon oil
2 teaspoons malt powder, optional
2 teaspoons salt
4 1/2 - 5 1/2 cups bread flour

Kettle Water
6 quarts water
2 tablespoons malt syrup or honey
1 teaspoon salt
Cornmeal, optional

Everything Topping
¼ cup dehydrated garlic
½ cup dehydrated onions
½ cup finely minced onions
¼ cup poppy seeds
Coarse salt

In a mixer bowl, whisk together water, yeast, and sugar. Let stand a couple of minutes to allow yeast to dissolve. Briskly whisk in in oil, malt and one cup of flour. Add salt, then most of remaining flour. Knead 10-12 minutes to make a very stiff dough. Cover with a tea towel and let dough rest on a board about 15 minutes.

Meanwhile, line two large baking sheets with baking parchment and sprinkle generously with corn meal. Fill a large pot two-thirds full with water; add the malt syrup and salt. Bring water to a gentle boil. Preheat oven to 450° F.

Divide dough into 10 sections and form into 10 inch long strips. Roll the ends together to seal and make a ring. Place on a very lightly floured surface near your stove. Let bagels rest 15 to 20 minutes.

Prepare two more baking sheets - line one with a kitchen towel, the other with parchment paper which has been sprinkled with cornmeal, if desired. Reduce water to simmer and add bagels a few at a time. Allow to come to surface and simmer thirty seconds. Turn over and cook other side about 45 seconds more. Place on prepared towel-lined baking sheet.

For Everything Topping, place the dehydrated onion and garlic in a small bowl and cover with steaming hot water. Let stand 5 minutes and then drain. Add fresh onion, poppy seed and oil to the bowl and mix ingredients. Deposit an equal amount of topping on each bagel. Dust with coarse salt.

Place in oven, reduce heat to 425° F. and bake until done, about 17-22 minutes, turning bagels once, when almost baked.

Makes 10

Baker's Tip #3

Cinnamon Raisin Whole-Wheat Bagels

Cinnamon is the core flavor in these bagels but not all cinnamon is created equal. I prefer a sweet-hot cinnamon and for that I blend half and half Chinese Cassia and Vietnamese Cinnamon for the best taste.

Cinnamon Raisin Whole-Wheat Bagels

...ething about a partially whole-wheat bagel along with some cinnamon that makes the most ...ng bagels. I add the cinnamon to the bagel by hand, gently kneading the dough to create a ...ized effect.

1 cup dark raisins, plumped
1 1/2 cups warm water
4 teaspoons instant yeast
2 tablespoons oil
2 tablespoons honey
¼ cup light brown sugar
1 1/4 cups whole-wheat flour
4 teaspoons cinnamon
1/4 cup light brown sugar
1 1/2 teaspoons salt
3 1/2 cups bread flour

Kettle Water

6 quarts water
2 tablespoons brown sugar

In a mixer bowl, whisk together the water and yeast and let stand a couple of minutes to allow yeast to swell and dissolve. Whisk in oil, honey, brown sugar, stirring to blend. Stir in whole-wheat flour, cinnamon and salt and blend well. Add in three cups of the white bread flour and begin kneading, 10-12 minutes, adding more flour as required to make a very firm but smooth dough.

Place dough on work surface, cover with a clean tea towel and allow to rest 10 minutes. Then divide into 10 portions. Form each portion into a rope about 10 inches long. Form into bagels by attaching ends together and rolling on board to lock ends. Let bagels rise about 20 minutes until they appear a little puffy. Preheat oven to 450° F.

Meanwhile fill a large pot two-thirds fill with water and add the brow... sugar. Bring water to a gentle boil. Prepare a large baking sheet by lini... with parchment paper. Place a few bagels at a time in boiling water... they come to the surface, turn them over and allow to cook on othe... another minute. Remove to baking sheet and place in oven, redu... to 425 degrees F. and bake until done, about 18-22 minutes.

Makes 10

The Legend of Montreal Bagels

Montreal may be the "Paris of the North" but just ask any American tourist who's ever been there ab... of this city's most special, renowned bagel! (Not to mention the other delights such as Montreal Smoked M... and legendary Poutine).

Montreal bagels are always made in a wood-fired bagel oven and are sweeter, enriched with honey, eggs, and oil, almost void of salt, and scaled smaller. Then they're simmered in a honey-laced water bath. The omission of salt makes the taste of the generous sesame seed coating really shine through. Overall, these are less dense than the traditional American bagels, unique well as memorable.

...gels here came to be developed exactly in this fashion is difficult to confirm. The recipe ...no doubt modelled after one or two immigrant families' bagel know-how and own ...hen these original family-run bagel stores came into existence. Over time, ...ed and expected bagels of this style and so the tradition continued. Some also ...s do not allow for wood-burning commercial ovens as they are a fire ...the dubious distinction of having great bagels and a slightly more

...bagel shops are still located in the more colourful, earthy ...d of product marketing except for the aroma of fresh ...ocation, and slightly less-than health board code of ...e-ups out the door all year long, even on the ...alongside hordes of Italian racing bikes and ...ix. In fact during Montreal winters, the ...scends. The intense heat of the wood oven together with the frigid cold of winter coats the bagel shops' windows with condensation and the display front reveals only a blurry gloss of deep amber-coloured bagels.

Making Montreal Bagels at Home (wherever home is)

I spent years studying various Montreal bagel makers and bakers, accessing, and learning. Then I would run home and, based on my observations, as well as conversations with local bagel makers, try batch after batch of homemade Montreal bagels. Finally, after many attempts, perfection! You might not have a wood bagel oven handy and that's part of the charm, but my home recipe for Montreal Bagels is a pretty close, if not perfect version of the bagel kingpin of Montreal.

Enjoy!

Baker's Tip #4

Montreal Bagels

Montreal Bagels are unique due to the honey in the boiling kettle water, and some malt and some egg inside. They also traditionally don't call for any salt but once you've had an authentic Montreal Bagel you won't go back!

Cinnamon Raisin Whole-Wheat Bagels

There's something about a partially whole-wheat bagel along with some cinnamon that makes the most tantalizing bagels. I add the cinnamon to the bagel by hand, gently kneading the dough to create a marbleized effect.

1 cup dark raisins, plumped
1 1/2 cups warm water
4 teaspoons instant yeast
2 tablespoons oil
2 tablespoons honey
¼ cup light brown sugar
1 1/4 cups whole-wheat flour
4 teaspoons cinnamon
1/4 cup light brown sugar
1 1/2 teaspoons salt
3 1/2 cups bread flour

Kettle Water

6 quarts water
2 tablespoons brown sugar

In a mixer bowl, whisk together the water and yeast and let stand a couple of minutes to allow yeast to swell and dissolve. Whisk in oil, honey, brown sugar, stirring to blend. Stir in whole-wheat flour, cinnamon and salt and blend well. Add in three cups of the white bread flour and begin kneading, 10-12 minutes, adding more flour as required to make a very firm but smooth dough.

Place dough on work surface, cover with a clean tea towel and allow to rest 10 minutes. Then divide into 10 portions. Form each portion into a rope about 10 inches long. Form into bagels by attaching ends together and rolling on board to lock ends. Let bagels rise about 20 minutes until they appear a little puffy. Preheat oven to 450° F.

Meanwhile fill a large pot two-thirds fill with water and add the brown sugar. Bring water to a gentle boil. Prepare a large baking sheet by lining with parchment paper. Place a few bagels at a time in boiling water. As they come to the surface, turn them over and allow to cook on other side another minute. Remove to baking sheet and place in oven, reduce heat to 425 degrees F. and bake until done, about 18-22 minutes.

Makes 10

The Legend of Montreal Bagels

Montreal may be the "Paris of the North" but just ask any American tourist who's ever been there about one of this city's most special, renowned bagel! (Not to mention the other delights such as Montreal Smoked Meat and legendary Poutine).

Montreal bagels are always made in a wood-fired bagel oven and are sweeter, enriched with honey, eggs, and oil, almost void of salt, and scaled smaller. Then they're simmered in a honey-laced water bath. The omission of salt makes the taste of the generous sesame seed coating really shine through. Overall, these are less dense than the traditional American bagels, unique as well as memorable.

How bagels here came to be developed exactly in this fashion is difficult to confirm. The recipe itself was no doubt modelled after one or two immigrant families' bagel know-how and own preferences when these original family-run bagel stores came into existence. Over time, Montrealers enjoyed and expected bagels of this style and so the tradition continued. Some also argue that other cities do not allow for wood-burning commercial ovens as they are a fire hazard, giving Montreal the dubious distinction of having great bagels and a slightly more relaxed fire code.

In Montreal, the finest, legendary bagel shops are still located in the more colourful, earthy parts of town and are scrupulously void of product marketing except for the aroma of fresh bagels on a wood hearth fire. Despite their location, and slightly less-than health board code of décor and hygiene, these bagel shops brag line-ups out the door all year long, even on the coldest, snowiest days. Double-spaced luxury cars, alongside hordes of Italian racing bikes and toney strollers are the norm as bagel addicts get their fix. In fact during Montreal winters, the bagel business booms as the outer temperature descends. The intense heat of the wood oven

Montreal Bagels

You can wait to visit Montreal or depend on Canadian relatives to tote some over the border (if you're stateside) or just try this authentic bagel recipe yourself. I've spent years perfecting this recipe, visiting and watching bagel makers at work - assessing techniques and the ingredients used in the many famous Montreal bagel landmarks such as The Bagel Factory on St. Viateur and the Fairmont Bagel Factory.

- 1 3/4 cups warm water
- 2 1/2 teaspoons instant yeast
- 5 tablespoons sugar
- 2 tablespoons beaten egg
- 3 tablespoons oil
- 1 tablespoon malt powder
- 1 1/2 teaspoons salt, optional
- 4 1/2 - 5 cups bread flour
- 1 1/2 cups sesame seed or poppy seeds

Kettle Water
- 6 quarts water
- 1/3 cup honey

In a mixer bowl, whisk together the water and yeast, and let stand a couple of minutes, allowing yeast to dissolve. Briskly whisk in sugar, beaten egg, vegetable oil, malt and fold in most of the flour. Knead on slow speed 10-12 minutes to form a stiff, smooth dough, begin kneading, 10-12 minutes, adding additional flour as required. Cover with a tea towel and let rest ten minutes. Preheat oven to 450° F.

Line one large baking sheet with a kitchen towel, the other with parchment paper. Fill a large pot two-thirds full with water and add the honey and salt. Bring water to a gentle boil. Meanwhile, divide in 12 sections and form into 10 inch strips. Form these into bagel rings and place on cookie sheet. Let rise 12-16 minutes until bagels are slightly puffed up.

Boil bagels about 1 1/2 minutes each, turning over once. Place on towel-lined sheet first to dry out. Then sprinkle very generously with sesame or poppy seeds. (Montreal Bagels are more seeded than regular bagels) and place on parchment lined sheet.

Place in oven; reduce heat to 425° F. Bake until done, about 15-22 minutes, turning bagels over once when they are just about done.

Makes 12

Baker's Tip #5

Caramel Apple Bagels

Bit of caramel and tangy apples, such as Cortland or McIntosh are best for this recipe because their flavor is a nice contrast in the bagel dough.

Caramel Apple Bagels

The quintessential fall and winter bagel, replete with butterscotch chips, caramel hunks and diced apples. How good are these? I traded some for regular bagels at my local bagel shop. The pros near fainted with delight!

2 cups warm water
2 1/2 teaspoons instant yeast
5-6 cups bread flour
2 tablespoons honey
3 tablespoons brown sugar
2 teaspoons salt
1 teaspoon malt powder, optional
Pinch cinnamon
1 cup butterscotch, caramel or white chocolate chips
4 cups diced, peeled apples
1 cup diced caramels

Kettle Water
6 quarts water
2 tablespoons honey
2 teaspoons salt

Finishing Touches
½ cup brown sugar
1/3 cup oatmeal

Line a doubled up baking sheet with parchment paper and set aside.

In a mixer bowl, hand whisk the water and yeast and let stand 2 minutes, Then briskly add in a cup of the flour, honey, brown sugar, salt, malt and cinnamon and blend well. Fold in most of the flour (all but 2 cups) to make a stiff dough. Attach dough hook and knead, 10-12 minutes adding more flour as required to make a very slick dough. Let rest 20 minutes, lightly covered in plastic wrap.

Meanwhile, heat fill a large pot two-thirds full with water, honey and salt and bring to a gentle boil. Press dough down and knead in the butterscotch chips, apples and caramels. If mixture gets wet and slack, dust in more flour. Let dough rest, lightly covered with plastic wrap, 15 minutes.

Gently deflate and then divide dough into 10-14 sections and cover lightly with a tea towel. Form each into an 8-10 inch rope. Press two ends together, and roll back and forth on a work surface to "lock" and form a ring or bagel. In a small bowl, mix the brown sugar and oatmeal.

Preheat oven to 450° F.

Place bagels in simmering water a few at a time and simmer, turning once, for about 3 minutes. Place boiled bagels on parchment-lined baking sheet. Dust the tops with brown sugar/oatmeal mixture. Place bagels back on baking sheet.

Bake until nicely browned on top side, turning once to brown undersides, about 15-20 minutes in total.

Makes 10-14

Baker's Tip #6

Dark Rye and Currant Pumpernickel Bagels

Dark rye means using stone-ground rye flour which includes all parts of the rye berry. These bagels also use a baker's caramel or Kitchen Bouquet which is essentially burnt sugar that is a colourant for pumpernickel breads.

Dark Rye and Currant Pumpernickel Bagels

A short sponge starter greatly enhances the flavor and texture of these fragrant rye bagels. Great for sweet and savory snacks, or topped with cheese with a cup of tea or coffee. Don't forget to buy coarse or dark rye flour.

Quick Sponge

1 cup warm water
1 tablespoon instant yeast
2 tablespoons caraway seeds
2 teaspoons malt powder or brown sugar
1 cup coarse or dark rye for pumpernickel flour
1/4 cup white bread flour

Dough

1/2 cup warm water
2 teaspoons baker's caramel or Kitchen Bouquet Gravy Browning
2 teaspoons salt
1/4 cup brown sugar
1/4 teaspoon cinnamon
2 1/2 to 3 cups white bread flour
1 cup currants, plumped and dried

Kettle Water

6 quarts water
1/3 cup brown sugar
1 teaspoon salt

For the sponge, an hour before making dough, mix together the water, yeast, caraway seeds, malt powder or sugar, rye flour, white bread flour and caraway seeds. Stir to make a thick gloppy mixture and let stand one hour.

To make the bagel dough, stir down sponge mixture and add (from Dough ingredients) water, baker's caramel, salt, sugar, cinnamon and most of white bread flour. Stir until dough can be kneaded and knead 10-12 minutes, adding in additional flour as required to make a stiff. Let rest a couple of minutes then press currants into the dough. Place dough in a bowl that has been generously sprayed with non-stick cooking spray. Cover with plastic wrap and let rise 30 minutes.

Divide dough into 10-12 portions and form each into a bagel.

Meanwhile, fill a large pot two-thirds filled with water, add the sugar and salt. Allow to come to a gentle boil.

Preheat oven to 450° F. Meanwhile, bring water and brown sugar to a boil. Prepare a large baking sheet by lining with parchment paper. Place a few bagels at a time in boiling water. As they rise to the surface, turn them over and allow them to cook on other side another minute. Remove to baking sheet and let dry briefly.

Bake until done (bagels will be nicely browned all over) 18-22 minutes.

Makes 8-10

Baker's Tip #7

Pumpkin Cranberry Bagels

Nothing is better than spunky pumpkin in a bagel! Use a pure pumpkin puree mix and not pie filling for these sumptuous autumn bagels. Make them mini for the Thanksgiving bread basket.

Pumpkin Cranberry Bagels

Like Thanksgiving in the round, these are simply amazing bagels: rustic and touched with a kiss of pumpkin spice, pumpkin puree, and a good smattering of dried cranberries. Feel free to swap in some whole-wheat flour if you like.

1 1/2 cup dried cranberries, plumped and dried
1 1/2 cups warm water
2 ¾ teaspoons instant yeast
2 tablespoons oil
3 tablespoons honey
1/3 cup light brown sugar, firmly packed
1 cup pumpkin puree
4 - 6 cups bread flour
1 3/4 teaspoons salt
1 ½ teaspoons pumpkin pie spice
1 teaspoon cinnamon

Kettle Water

6 quarts water
1/3 cup brown sugar
1 teaspoon salt

Plump cranberries by covering them with very hot water and allow them to sit for five minutes. Drain and use a paper towel to dry thoroughly. Set aside. Stack two baking sheets together and line the top one with parchment paper.

In a mixer bowl, whisk together the water, yeast, oil, honey and brown sugar, stirring to dissolve yeast and sugar. Stir in pumpkin puree. Stir in half of the flour, salt, pumpkin pie spice and cinnamon and blend well. Add more flour and begin kneading, 10-12 minutes, adding more flour as required to make a very stiff dough but remember to add cranberries about half way through the kneading period. Place dough on work surface, cover with a clean tea towel and let rest 10 minutes; then divide into 10 portions. Form each portion into a rope about 10 inches long. Form into bagels by attaching ends together and rolling on board to lock ends. Let bagels rise about 15 minutes until they appear a little puffy.

Preheat oven to 450° F. Meanwhile, fill a large pot two-thirds full with water, add the brown sugar and bring to a gentle boil. Prepare a large baking sheet by lining with parchment paper. Place a few bagels at a time in boiling water. As they rise to the surface, turn them over and allow them to cook on other side another minute. Remove to baking sheet and let dry briefly. Dust with some cinnamon.

Bake until done (bagels will be nicely browned all over) 18-22 minutes.

Makes 10

Baker's Tip #8

Spelt & Whole Wheat and Flax Seed Bagels

I love grainy tasting things and the flour mix and seeds in this bagel recipe makes them extra nutritious and they toast up especially fragrant.

Spelt & Whole Wheat and Flax Seed Bagels

Spelt is one of those especially highly nutritious, ancient wheats. These are crusty, chewy, moist and full of flavour, and heart-healthy affairs. There is just enough whole-wheat and spelt to be extra-healthy and enough unbleached white bread flour to ensure the bagels are not dry.

Dough

2 cups warm water

2 1/2 teaspoons instant yeast

2 cups organic whole-wheat flour

2 tablespoons honey

2 teaspoons salt

1 teaspoon malt powder, optional

1/3 cup ground flax seeds

1/4 cup bran flakes or natural bran

1 cup white or regular spelt flour

2 1/2 - 3 1/2 cups unbleached white bread flour

Sesame seeds

Flax Seeds

Kettle Water

6 quarts water

2 tablespoons honey

2 teaspoons salt

Stack two baking sheets together and line the top one with parchment paper.

In a mixer bowl, briskly whisk together water and yeast. Fold in the whole-wheat flour and then briskly whisk in the honey, salt, malt, flax seeds, bran, spelt, (already added) whole-wheat flour and half of the white flour. Knead 10-12 minutes, adding in more as required to make a very slick dough. Let rest 20 minutes, lightly covered in plastic wrap.

Fill a large pot two-thirds filled with water and add the honey and salt. Allow to come to a gentle boil. Divide dough into 12-14 sections. Form each into an 8-10 inch rope. Press two ends together, and roll back and forth on a work surface to "lock" and form a ring or bagel. Have a bowl of sesame seeds nearby. Preheat oven to 450° F.

Place bagels in simmering water a few at a time and simmer, turning once, for about 3 minutes. Place bagels on parchment-lined baking sheet. When they are all done, toss them well in sesame seeds, dust on some flax seeds and then put the bagels back on baking sheet. Bake until nicely browned, turning once, about 15-20 minutes.

Makes 12-14

Baker's Tip #9

Rosemary Sea Salt Bagels

Use a coarse sea salt which is a large crystal, not opaque such as a pretzel salt, for these garden fresh bagels which take well to cream cheese.

Rosemary Sea Salt Bagels

Who doesn't like that fragrant combination of sea salt and rosemary on a bagel? This is a trending flavour that probably will become a deserved classic.

1 1/2 cups warm water
1 tablespoon instant yeast
1 tablespoon sugar
1 tablespoon oil
2 teaspoons malt powder, optional
4 1/2 - 5 1/2 cups bread flour
2 teaspoons salt
1/2 teaspoon dried rosemary or
2 teaspoons minced fresh rosemary
Coarse sea salt

Kettle Water

6 quarts water
1 teaspoon salt

In a mixer bowl, whisk together water, yeast, and sugar. Let stand a couple of minutes to allow yeast to dissolve. Quickly whisk in the oil, malt and one cup of flour. Add salt, rosemary and most of remaining flour. Knead 10-12 minutes, adding in more flour if required to make a very stiff dough. Cover with a tea towel and let dough rest on a board about 15 minutes.

Meanwhile, line two large baking sheets with parchment paper and sprinkle generously with corn meal. Fill a large pot two-thirds full with water and bring water to a gentle boil. Preheat oven to 450° F.

Divide in 10 sections and form into 10 inch long strips. Roll the ends together to seal and make a ring. Place on a very lightly floured surface near your stove. Let bagels rest 15 to 20 minutes. Bagels should have a half proof and should rise halfway or appear puffy.

Reduce water to simmer and add bagels a few at a time. Allow to come to surface and simmer thirty seconds. Turn over and cook other side about 45 seconds more. Place on prepared towel lined baking sheet. Leave plain or sprinkle on some sea salt and a light dusting of rosemary.

Place in oven, reduce heat to 425° F. and bake until done, about 17-22 minutes, turning bagels once, when almost baked.

Makes 10

Baker's Tip #10

Stuffed Cheddar Cheese Bagels

Something about the appeal of bread and cheese is classically loved so use a quality, preferably medium or sharp cheddar cheese in these or experiment with different cheeses like Asiago or Feta.

Stuffed Cheddar Cheese Bagels

What could be better than big, rustic, hearth-baked bagels, unless they are stuffed with sharp cheddar cheese. These are extra chewy and feature a molten river of cheese.

1 3/4 cups warm water
1 tablespoon instant yeast
1 tablespoon sugar
2 tablespoons beaten egg
3 tablespoons oil
1 teaspoon malt, optional
2 teaspoons salt
4 1/2 - 5 cups bread flour
12 ounces sharp orange cheddar, shredded
Sesame seeds

Kettle Water

6 quarts water
1/4 cup honey
2 teaspoons salt

In a mixer bowl, whisk water with yeast and allow to stand a few minutes. Briskly whisk in the sugar, beaten egg, vegetable oil, malt, salt and fold in most of the flour.

Knead 10-12 minutes, adding in more flour as required to form stiff dough. Cover with a tea towel or inverted bowl and let rest ten minutes. Line one large baking sheet with a kitchen towel and another one with parchment paper.

Fill a large pot two-thirds full with water, add honey and salt. Bring water to a gentle boil. Meanwhile, divide in 12 sections and flatten each into an oval. Place about 1/3 cup cheese down the middle length of the dough. Roll up into a roll or log, then shape and seal to make a ring. Place on cookie sheet. Let rise 12-16 minutes until bagels are very slightly puffed up.

Preheat oven to 450° F. Boil bagels about 1 1/2 minutes each, turning over once. Place on towel lined sheet first to dry out. Then sprinkle generously with sesame seeds and some of the reserved cheddar. Place on parchment lined sheet. Place in oven, reduce heat to 425 F. Bake until done, about 15-22 minutes, turning bagels over once when they are just about done.

Makes 12

Baker's Tip #11

Wild Blueberry Bagels

Frozen blueberries work best in these bagels because they hold their shape in baking but wild blueberries have a special fresh-country taste. I use a combination of wild and cultivated blueberries in this wonderful recipe.

Wild Blueberry Bagels

These are actually made with cultivated blueberries but they are indeed wildly blue and delicious. Something about a rustic bagel dough as a holding pen for pudgy purple blueberries is fantastic to both behold and eat.

1 ½ cups warm water
2 ¾ teaspoons instant yeast
2 tablespoons oil
3 tablespoons honey
1 3/4 teaspoons salt
4 - 6 cups bread flour
1 ½ cups frozen blueberries

Kettle Water

6 quarts water
1/3 cup brown sugar
1 teaspoon salt

Stack two baking sheets together and line the top one with parchment paper.

In a mixer bowl, whisk together the water and yeast and allow to stand 2-3 minutes. Briskly whisk in the oil, honey, salt and a cup of the flour. Add more flour and begin kneading. Knead 10-12 minutes, adding more flour as required to make a very stiff dough. Add or press in blueberries to the dough gently so as not to break up blueberries.

Place dough on work surface, cover with a clean tea towel and allow to rest lo minutes. Then divide into 8, lo, or 12 portions (8 for larger bagels, 10 for medium, or 12 for small). Form each portion into a rope about 10 inches long. Form into bagels by attaching ends together and rolling on board to lock ends. Let bagels rise about 15 minutes until they appear a little puffy.

Preheat oven to 450° F.

Meanwhile, fill a large pot two-thirds full with water, brown sugar and bring to a gentle boil. Prepare a large baking sheet by lining with parchment paper. Place a few bagels at a time in boiling water. As they rise to the surface, turn them over and allow them to cook on other side another minute. Place on baking sheet as you remove bagels.

Bake until done (bagels will be nicely browned all over) and turn over once for a few minutes to complete baking, 18-22 minutes.

Makes 10-12

Bakers Tip #12

Twisted Bagel Bread

Bagel dough also makes a great loaf of bread and this recipe makes a rustic bread that is as good fresh as it is toasted. It also keeps well.

Twisted Bagel Bread

Bagel dough fashioned into a twisted loaf, stuffed with golden Vidalia onions and roasted garlic. This is an exceptional bread in every way and it causes a 'wow' at first glance. It's also a great sandwich loaf and makes wonderful toast.

2 1/2 cups warm water
5 teaspoons instant yeast
1 tablespoon sugar
1 teaspoon dry malt powder or malt syrup, optional *
4 tablespoons honey
2 teaspoons salt
2 tablespoons oil
6 to 7 cups bread flour
Rye flour or cornmeal for dusting

Garlic Onion Topping

2 tablespoons oil
1 very large Vidalia onion, coarsely diced
2 large whole bulbs of garlic, coarsely minced
3 tablespoons poppy seeds

Finishing Touches

Egg wash
Coarse salt

In a mixer bowl, whisk together the water, yeast and sugar. Stir in (malt powder), honey, salt, and oil. Add most of flour to make a stiff dough, and knead for 10-12 minutes, adding in additional flour if required. Shape dough into a ball and place in a greased bowl. Insert bowl into a large plastic bag and allow to rise until almost doubled (in a very cool place - refrigerator, garage) for about 2 hours. Meanwhile, make the topping.

For the Garlic Onion Topping, in a non-stick skillet, slowly sauté the onions in the oil, over medium-low heat. When almost golden and softened, add in the garlic and cook to soften (but not brown or burn) the garlic. Remove to a bowl and add the poppy seeds.

Gentle deflate dough. Divide into three portions and flatten each one. Fill with 1/3 each of the onion garlic filling. Roll to tuck in filling and then roll to make each portion a rope or braid. Braid the three ropes together and twist into a circle and place in prepared pan. Brush with egg wash and then sprinkle with any filling that fell out and with some coarse salt. Cover and let rise 45-60 minutes until not quite doubled in size. Cover lightly in plastic wrap. Stack two baking sheets together and line the top one with parchment paper. Preheat oven to 375° F.

Bake for 30 minutes at 375° F and then reduce heat to 350° F and finish baking until

well-browned (another 25 to 35 minutes).

Makes one large loaf

Baker's Tip #13
Old Fashioned Onion Bialys

Bialys should be in their own food group and illustrate another way that you can use bagel dough. Bialys are simply bagel dough, formed differently and they aren't boiled before baking.

Old Fashioned Onion Bialys

Bialys are the bagel's first cousin. It's a disk of bagel dough with a slight depression in its center, topped with diced onions and poppy seeds. Bialys are amazingly rustic, chewy and addictive. If you like bagels, you'll love bialys!

Dough
1 1/2 cups warm water
5 teaspoons instant yeast
5 teaspoons sugar
5 - 5 1/2 cups bread flour
2 1/2 teaspoons salt

Topping
1 cup finely minced fresh onion
2 tablespoons vegetable oil
1 1/2 tablespoons poppy seeds
1 tablespoon coarse sea salt

Finishing Touches
Cornmeal for baking sheet (approximately 1/4 cup)
Egg, beaten with 2 tablespoons water

In a mixer bowl, whisk together water yeast and sugar. Stir in one cup of the flour and salt. Add most of remaining flour and stir with a wooden spoon to make a soft mass. Attach dough hook and knead on slow 10-12 minutes, adding in more flour as required. Allow dough to rest, covered with a tea towel for about 45 minutes. Meanwhile, line two large baking sheets with baking parchment and lightly sprinkle with corn meal.

Preheat oven to 450° F.

Prepare topping by covering onions with hot water and allow to soak for 15 minutes. Drain, toss with oil and poppy seeds. Set aside.

Deflate dough and divide in two. Divide each half section of dough into six equal pieces. Allow dough to rest ten minutes. Roll or stretch each portion into a 5 -7 inch oval or circle. Be careful not to overwork the dough. Place bialys on prepared baking sheets. Lightly glaze outer perimeter with egg wash. Spoon on about two teaspoons of prepared onion topping and a little bit of coarse salt (optional). Cover with a floured tea towel and allow to rise 30-40 minutes or until puffy.

Bake until golden brown (25-30 minutes). If bialys brown too fast, reduce heat to 425 F. For thicker bialys (good for sandwiches) allow to rise longer. For thin bialys, reduce rising period.

Makes 12-16

Acknowledgements

Senior Editors and Proof Readers

Wendy Berman, Jan Hirsch, Phyllisa Goldenberg, Sherri Seidmon

Recipe Testers

The following people graciously volunteered their time, energy, and ingredients in testing the recipes. I can't thank them enough. They ensured my recipes are exacting and as accurate and easy to replicate as possible.

Louise Allen	Karyl Barron
Wendy Berman	Uli Cotter
Diane DiVittorio	Susan Hatch
Jan Hirsch	Joyce Leitman
Janet Gardner	Phyllisa Goldenberg
Sherri Seidmon	Linda Sterling

Bonus Recipes!
3-Months Free Access to Betterbaking.com!

Please join me on this journey as we embark on the pathway of a baker's dozen of great bagels! I wish you great success with your baking, as well as warm happy memories, as you much and crunch your way through this rich collection. And don't forget; just email me at marcygoldman01@gmail or via www.betterbaking.com with proof of your cookbook purchase to obtain your free 3-months of all-recipe access to Betterbaking.com.

Other books by Marcy Goldman
Available on Amazon, Indigo and fine bookstores everywhere

www.ingramcontent.com/pod-product-compliance
Lightning Source LLC
Chambersburg PA
CBHW081758100526
44592CB00015B/2486